Holding up Half the Sky

Rosemary Mitchell
&
Hannah Stone

Indigo Dreams Publishing

First Edition: Holding up Half the Sky
First published in Great Britain in 2019 by:
Indigo Dreams Publishing
24, Forest Houses
Halwill
Beaworthy
Devon
EX21 5UU

www.indigodreams.co.uk

Rosemary Mitchell and Hannah Stone have asserted their rights under the Copyright, Designs and Patents Act 1988 to be identified as the authors of this work.
©2019

ISBN 978-1-912876-06-8

British Library Cataloguing in Publication Data. A CIP record for this book can be obtained from the British Library.

Designed and typeset in Palatino Linotype by Indigo Dreams.
Cover: Suffragette dress, 1914 (rayon & paper), created by Leonora Cohen (1873-1978) Copyright: Leeds Museums and Galleries (Leeds Art Gallery). Gift from Leonora Cohen, 1967/Bridgeman Images. Photographed by Norman Taylor.
Printed and bound in Great Britain by 4edge Ltd
www.4edge.co.uk
Papers used by Indigo Dreams are recyclable products made from wood grown in sustainable forests following the guidance of the Forest Stewardship Council.

To the British Suffrage campaigners of 1918

Acknowledgements

Macrina was first published in *Noble Dissent*, ed. Rebecca Bilkau (Beautiful Dragons, 2017).

Patricia was first published in *Perfect Timing* (Createspace/Wordspace, 2014).

Umm Hoda was first published in *Lodestone* (Stairwell Books, 2016).

A selection of the texts included here was performed as part of the Writing on Air Festival broadcast by East Leeds Chapel FM in April 2017.

We extend great gratitude to Oz Hardwick for supporting the project and for invaluable editorial input.

CONTENTS

Regina 9

Anonymous Figure, Ashmolean Museum 11

Macrina 12

The Empress Theodora, from her Bath 13

Mary to Zosimas 14

Syrian Mary and her Fallible Uncle 16

A Troubled Seer Writes to Bernard of Clairvaux 18

A Shewing in Which I am Nourished by Milk from Jesus'
Breasts 19

British Library MS Additional 61823: a Partial Chronology 20

The Duchess's Double: On the effigy of Alice Chaucer, Duchess
of Suffolk 21

Jeanne of Arc to her English Accusers 22

Queen Anne commends herself to Saint Margaret of Antioch.... 24

1544: Her Grace, in a Table 25

On Vermeer's Christ in the House of Martha and Mary 27

Receipt Book of Lady Cleavage of Combe, for the Year of Our
Lord, 1792 28

Closed Monday, Winter Months 31

Collection 33

The Conference Reception is Held in the Isabella Stewart
Gardner Museum 35

Rich Bride, or Christening Cake: Mrs Beeton Bakes 37

Pioneer Woman, or Prairie Queen 38

The Three Maries 39

A Say in Things 40

Archaeology of a Sort 43

Fenwick Lawson, Pietà, 1974-81, Elm 45

Patricia 46

Umm Hoda 47

Sacrament...49
We are not fools..50
Sally Yates to a Malefactor of Great Wealth, or Speaking Truth
to Power 51
Life-Cycle: on My Late Mother's Charm Bracelet 52

Afterword..53
Notes..54

Holding up
Half the Sky

Regina

Alas! Regina, my love, my wife, my queen!
You had a Celtic name I could not say
when first I purchased you, amid
the soft southern hills of this far-spread
Britannia. The Syrian girls I knew, dark-haired,
with eyes like glistening olives, were dusky-fair
pillars in Palmyra. You paled beside them.
But your storm-green eyes, changing like
northern seas, the angular jut
of your chin, a dauntless cliff, and the
uncertain shades in the forests of
your hair enchanted me. You had no words
I recognised, but there was a hard and salty
magic in your voice. Bride in this flowery desert
of the north, my slave commanded me, being queenly.
A perfect pearl which the diver finds
only once beneath the wave in a watery
lifetime. We came north to this wall,
for business sake – I being a banner-maker
to the Emperor's army. These rigid Romans still
yearn for dominion, planting their flags and feet
in all the world's wild corners. These lands tripped them up,
of course. This is an ever-shifting space
of winding streams, misty moors, and wild woods.
A land like you, my love: untamed.
To discipline this puzzling place, these soldiers built
a wall, on which I freed you, saw you fly
like a falcon rising in the winds. It's where I wed you,
too, and watched you die, slow gasping in your pain.
And now a Roman-handed sculptor tries to fix your image
on your tomb. I said to him – this slave was my Zenobia,
more conquering than the sun, and pale, mysterious
as the moon. Shape her here in stone for evertime.

He makes you now a prim Roman matron, spinning wool
and showing your jewel box with a smirk of pride.
By the gods of your strange land, this is not you!
You were your own jewel, and mine too; and to
my poor southern limbs, chilled by winter winds,
you were as warm as a woollen cloak. When the mason
is gone, I will smite away this simpering stone face,
and restore some jot, a *qal,* of unmasked you.

Rosemary Mitchell

Anonymous Figure, Ashmolean Museum

Curators of the temporary display
have suggested possible interpretations
of the two figures exhibited.
Goddess or Woman? they invite us to speculate.
The Goddess Aphrodite (Venus),
or a young woman dressed as her,
holds up a comb and mirror.
The statue dates from between AD200 and 230,
probably comes from north-west Turkey;
it's moulded from terracotta.
She's placed beside a *plastercast (1883):*
upper part of a marble relief.
King Antiochus I of Commegne
clasps the right hand of Hercules.

The monarch is clean-shaven;
boasts a coronet of clinging leaves,
and he's elaborately attired.
A text on the rear of the original statue
proclaims him to be *a friend to the Greeks and Romans.*
He's shaking hands with the *son of Zeus,*
who, being semi-divine, wears no robes.
Their neighbour stands, supported by cherubs.
She needs no emperor's new clothes to impress.
Broad-hipped, small-breasted,
she attends to her tresses.
Even a goddess might want to look her best.
I peer beyond her mirror,
and try to look her in the eye.

Hannah Stone

Macrina

*She should not be passed over in silence and her life rendered
ineffective...*
— St. Gregory of Nyssa.

No, I will not.
God gave me choices when he took
the man I was to marry,
and I will not lie down beneath another,
and watch my proved belly swell.
I will bind up my heart
in place of leaking breasts,
and mother those brothers of mine.
Ah, for all their philosophy, they can find
no word for me but bastardized masculinities.
They envy my 'manly soul', praise me
for fathering their orphaned selves.

I will not rouse the skivvy from her thin sleep,
but let her rest. I'll take the yeast,
crumble its humility into flour
then wait. And wait.

They rose, and blessed me
for guarding and forming their piety.
I left them to shape their futures,
punching out their doctrines,
and when they come, from time to time,
wearied and dusty from the world,
they eat the bread I've baked.
I will not waste the crumbs.

Hannah Stone

The Empress Theodora, from her Bath

I have been told the daughters of Rachel are required,
by priestly tradition,
to immerse themselves for cleansing
after their monthly courses.

Blood never bothered me,
neither dripping from my *,
nor shedding it, by sword or dagger.

I choose this perfumed pool each day
to wash away the slobber and spent seed;
though imperial, my spouse splatters his spittle
when he embraces me, and **, it is true.

They are rash, those courtiers who chide me
for lingering in my bath.
If I wished, I could ***.
They should remember who pays their wage.

Hey, girl, bring more hot water now,
or I'll tell the slave master to ****.

---

*   the translation is obscene, but indicates the female pudenda
**   a lacuna in all manuscripts
***   blemish due to water damage; possibly 'remove (or curtail) their
appendages'
**** phrase removed as offensive to common decency

Hannah Stone

Mary to Zosimas

on lichaman dead and on gaste libbende
(dead in body and living in the spirit):
> Hugh Magennis, ed. *The Old English Life of Saint Mary of Egypt*
> (Exeter Medieval Texts and Studies, 2002).

Brother Zosimas, read this message I have left for you
scratched into parched earth by my cave.
Have mercy on the remains of the harlot Mary;
commit her carcass to the earth, let dust return to dust.
And pray for me, as I shall for you, remembering
your many mercies towards me.
If you are too feeble from fasting
to gouge out my grave, then do not fear
the lioness, who waits with curled claws
to scoop a pit wherein you may bury
the shrouded shell of a woman
whose sins scorched her soul as black as any Ethiopian.
Her skin and soul were matched in darkness,
burned while wandering seven times seven years
under the desert sun, scorched till the coarse sand
became the fuller's earth to cleanse her reeking limbs.
For now I am *on lichaman dead and on gaste libbende.*

Remember me to your brother monks;
remind them how my story shows
the glories of God's compassion to the penitent,
that one against whose lascivious deeds
the very doors of mother church stood closed
was moved to beg the Holy Virgin
to hear a wanton woman's prayer;
how, shriven, I stole away to hide in the wilderness,
where first you saw me, and were frit half to death
at the seeming apparition that was me. How, seeing
beyond my unworthiness, you begged of me a blessing,
which benison I craved from you, dear brother,

whose kindness had already covered my shameful parts
with half your meagre garment, for we both strove to be
on lichaman dead and on gaste libbende.

Above our heads the risen moon radiated a wan light,
its silver disc reflected below our feet, shimmering
on the dark waters. From my uplifted hand
God's power poured forth, paving
a safe passage for my sinful feet, so on the far side
of the Jordan river I could depart from you,
further from habitation,
submitting my fiery lust to the desert's furnace,
purifying the soiled flesh which once embraced
the wicked needs of so many men, so that now
I am *on lichaman dead and on gaste libbende.*

Then, I blessed the river with the sign
of our Lord's passion, and now, dear Zosimas,
bless me with your tears, then cover
the white wool of my hair
with handfuls of golden grains,
so that beneath the desert's sandy soil
my mortal limbs may rest at last,
while my bright soul is borne up by angels
into the refreshing presence of Christ Jesu.
This I beg, good Zosimas, for we are both
on lichaman dead and on gaste libbende.

Hannah Stone

Syrian Mary and her Fallible Uncle

In a town in a hot climate lived Abraham, with his niece Mary, an unsullied girl. He built a home for them both, with rooms inside for himself, and an outer apartment for her, surrounded by a garden, where she grew flowers, and put down fragments of food for the birds. The wall between them was pierced by a window, so he could watch over her safety, and she could alert him to all her needs.

Abraham invited a guest, in appearance a monk, but beneath his simple garments rose up all the passions of a man. He spied young Mary, desired her beauty, and soon he thrust his way inside her fortress. His lust satisfied, the devious man slunk away, leaving the young woman to her lot. A dark cloud overlaid her heart; shame flooded her being and she fled her home. Abraham went out into the garden and saw the broken stems of flowers crushed in her flight. Bereft and guilty, he kept lonely vigils, tried in vain to sleep and, when he did, dreams tormented him.

He saw a serpent slithering in the garden where once the maid had tended her plants. It seized a white dove, swallowed it whole and wound its way back towards its foetid lair. Abraham awoke, drenched in sweat, rigid with horrid excitement. He slept again; the serpent came once more, sliding over the threshold into his own room. In his dream he recoiled in dread as the wily worm approached, and slid its head beneath the old man's feet. The reptile writhed; its entrails split and spat from its scaly prison a dove, which fluffed up its feathers in the fresh air, and fluttered heavenwards.

By this sign, the old man knew his niece was still alive. He closed up the house and locked the garden gate, shod himself with stout shoes, and went in search of his lost girl. For two years he wandered, encouraged sometimes by the curl of a feather tumbling in the road's dust. His nights were now empty of visions; the eyes of his mind were blind, yet still he searched for his forsaken kinswoman. Grief gnawed his guts as he recalled how he had opened his house to a trusted man whose corrupted intentions had seduced her purity.

At length he came to a city strange to him, where after many months of the wind's music and the patter of his stumbling pace, the clamour of merchants bruised his ear; rich smells from cooking pots awoke his appetites. Bold girls with bright eyes called to him, coiled their arms round his weary shoulders. A wench pulled aside a rich embossed curtain, welcomed him into her sanctuary, but as he approached her couch, she started, and greeted him by his name. It was the lost one, found.

Uncle and niece united in chaste embrace, and, covered by darkness, they left the city, retraced the long route back to safe enclosure. Abraham placed his precious penitent inside their home, where through the window in the wall she could look out on him, and bless him every day for sheltering her recovered virtue from marauding men. Above the shady trees of the garden birds circled, and called to each other.

Hannah Stone

A Troubled Seer Writes to Bernard of Clairvaux

Reverend Father Bernard, forgive an anxious woman for disturbing you again. In my last letter, I gave thanks that in an effeminate age you shone as a vanquisher and a truly brave man. I am unschooled in external matters, but when I saw you, in a vision, I understood you to be an eagle who dared look into the sun. Again, I weep that I am so timorous; I rail against my frailty, craving the strength of your virtue. I am greatly troubled by this new vision which has appeared to me through the inspiration of divine mystery; it is not revealed to me through the eyes of flesh. I bless the womb of Mary in which the Father of all, in a sweet greening, laid his Word to suck flesh, confined in this small house like honey that is walled around with comb. In my vision, a pierced womb with neither feet nor legs rested on the altar. Light streamed from its wounds, and many children moved in the air around it, like fishes in water. Angels assisted them to enter the womb, where their soiled flesh was peeled from them and the serene light coalesced, reclothing them in white garments. I am troubled to explain this, Reverend Father, wretched as I am – and the more wretched for bearing the name of woman – I beg you, as one of Adam's type from whose rib I splintered off, tell me what I have seen. Give me words to share my vision.

Hannah Stone

**A Shewing in Which I am Nourished by Milk from Jesus'
Breasts**

In this shewing I know that God rejoices to be our mother.
He whose sinews were knit together inside the innocent Virgin
makes himself the womb of our salvation,
forming our limbs and fleshing them out
till, too cramped to rest, we urge to be birthed.
Then he suffers the sharpest labour pangs.
Pain pierces him, stabbing like the nails
that pin him to the tree.

And I see that our sinful selves do not slither into the world
as through a woman's splayed legs;
rather, we are shepherded in and out of his blessed bosom
through the holes made in his sweet side
by Roman spear thrusts. His wounds
are an open gate, so we can enter him, and find union,
just as he longs to find his home deep in our being.

And I see Jesus lift my infant body up to suckle
at his breasts, grasp his gushing nipple thrust
into my mouth, so I can suck the flow of his marvellous love,
nourishing me in my first Eucharist.

Hannah Stone

British Library MS Additional 61823: a Partial Chronology

c. 1373: Margery born to Brunham, Mayor of King's Lynn.

c. 1393: Margery marries John Kempe.

1413-1433: She bears fourteen children. Takes a vow of chastity, which is approved by a bishop, and accepted by her husband. She weeps a great deal; fabricates a hair shirt from sacking procured from a malt drying kiln. She continues to weep. She travels, sometimes without a chaperone. She visit anchoress Julian, in Norwich, and her tears are confirmed as holy. She visits Venice, Assisi, Rome, Jerusalem, Santiago de Compostela, Prussia. Also Great Yarmouth, Hull, Ely. She kisses lepers on the lips. She interviews Bishops and archbishops. Is arrested and examined. Is arrested and accused – of witchcraft, heresy; her learning is cause for suspicion. She weeps. She writes (maybe). Is arrested and imprisoned. She writes that she would rather lie with God than her husband. She writes about family, fashion, lust, liking, corruption, ecclesiastical matter. Plants. She fills her soul with the Company of Heaven.

Sometime after 1438: she dies.

Scribes copy out her book. Better scribes re-copy it. Salthow's fair copy is placed in the library at Mount Grace priory, North Riding of Yorkshire.

1539: The monastery is dissolved.

1600: Silence. Her book lies still.

1700: Silence. Her book is lost.

1800: Silence. Her book is dumb.

1934: Hope Emily Allen discovers Margery's Book, among the affairs of the Butler-Bowden family in Lancashire. It is catalogued by the British Library.

Hope smiles through Margery's tears.

Hannah Stone

The Duchess's Double: On the effigy of Alice Chaucer, Duchess of Suffolk

Pilgrim, pause – and wonder at my state:
wimpled, with my coronet, my pious palms
pressed in prayer, and all around me angels, obsequious
attendants, a retinue arranged and ripe for heaven.
True, one is curling round my ear, beneath my canopy,
whispering a cheeky caution against pride.
Others weep dutifully, wet sentinels on the side
of my tomb, spindly-legged and golden-winged,
their shields boasting my worldly pedigree, even as
they shoot me up to heaven's gate. There's where I'm sped,
for I have built God's house below, upon this patch
of clay. My alms-house, my scholars, and my poet
sing shrilly up to God of my good works
in bright red brick and brighter words in book.
So when I beat upon His door, dare He refuse?

But still, if you kneel, pilgrim, and steal a look
under the angels' feet and through a screen,
you'll see me dead, and stripped, and bare,
chicken-necked, my cheeks sunk in, and
my mouth a horrid hole, my withered
breasts melted on the ripples of my ribs.
This, too, is my estate, as if I'd watched and wasted
a century in the desert with St John. Above my face,
an image floats on which I fix my eyeless, empty gaze:
the Queen of Heaven, as she quickens with the Christ,
looks down on me. Perhaps I am comforted.
Pilgrim, pass on. You too will come to this.

Rosemary Mitchell

Jeanne of Arc to her English Accusers

Do not make me put on a woman's garb.
I who have worn the armour of God
and marched for France. I am not as once
I was, a peasant girl, wandering with
her goats in green pastures. No, I am now
the tool, the fool of God, who graciously
sent his saints to sit in my head, and speak
to me. *Save France,* they said. *These Englishmen
set sacrilegious feet on God's demesne.
Rise up, Jeanne, and drive them out.* I did not
wish to hear such voices. But, besieged and
beaten by them, I yielded then, and sped
first to my earthly lord, no angel he, then
to my country's king, the doleful dauphin,
turning as terrible as an army
in banners. God raised up men, and threw down
you English. You do not forget the walls
of Orleans, I think. God gave me wings
and now he gives me words. I am not wise
yet I can defy you still. Be sure
this woman's robe cannot arrest the work
of Revelation. For now I am clothed
with the Sun. I mean to burn, a flame
which you cannot put out with trials, and courts,
and cries of *wicked woman, cursèd whore.*
Once I was a little cowed by your pride
of rank, and your unshaken conviction
that our land was yours by some ancient right.
But the saints shook my head, reminding me
that you are mortal men – and I am God's.
Go home, English lords. Hearken to me, else doom
will fall on you, a weak mad king, and then
a war of kin on kin. Be wise; go home.

Your faces say you still want France,
though she were set in hell, and you cast
down upon her. Why then, I bid you all farewell.
Place me now upon your pyre, and set
a torch to it. Let me burn. For the saints
still speak. They say: *she does the will of God,*
and speed me on to him. But you Englishmen,
God sees, and judges, and with a searing sword
Saint Michael comes to burn you to your bones.

Rosemary Mitchell

Queen Anne commends herself to Saint Margaret of Antioch

Lonely Queen Anne, contemplative in her chambers, sits in the oriel window. Here the sun raises a ruddy glow on her tawny velvet sleeves, and the pearls in her bodice and her crescent hood shine like a promise of redemption. In her Book of Hours (Sarum usage), she gazes upon the sedate image of Saint Margaret. In yellow margins, she finds goldfinches considering the uncertain pleasures of ripe strawberries, fresh in their rosy innocence, but promiscuous in pips, seeding in sin. *A serpent lurks here*, she thinks. *Better the unpretending violets, humble even to death, yet priestly in their purple robes. Or the three-coloured pansies, which speak the Trinity. Or even the bitter thistle, crown on Christ's head.* She marks that one of the finches is plucking out a fly from that green prickly thorn, and shivers. The babe in her womb shifts a little. Their two hearts beat as one, once, before her eye is caught by a caterpillar, curling above the saint.

She glances through the glass, and sees, in the summer garden, the king clad in gold and green, pausing at a limpid pool, with a demure, horse-faced damsel at his side. *Her name is Jane*, the queen recalls. She wears a dated gable hood, shielding puffy cheeks, an expression like an empty page, awaiting the scribe's pen and the artist's brush. In a twist of anguish, the queen turns to the saint. Unconsciously mimicking Margaret, she looks to her Book, eschewing the picture beyond the pane. The saint's face is pale, her chin and nose pointed, and her forehead plucked and shaven. Prepared for her Passion, she clutches her golden cross, while her psalter's pages rise, ripple, and rustle in the fiery breath of the dog-like dragon behind her skirts. He turns the regal canopy above her hood a blood-bright scarlet. *Peace*, says Anne to herself: *he may swallow her, true, but not for long.* Already and always, it seems, she re-emerges, resurrected. The queen heaves a sigh, and gently strokes her swollen belly.

Rosemary Mitchell

1544: Her Grace, in a Table

Item: pd to one John that drue her grace in a table
(Frederic Madden, ed. *Privy Purse Expenses of the Princess Mary*, 1831)

A tablet square, with azure field, charged
with a woman's bust *affronti*, eyes *dexter*,
chaperonné, hood edged in rubies and pearls,
veil sable. A bodice *tenné*, diaper *argent*, sleeves
sanguine, counter-salient, over undersleeves *blanc*,
edged sable, with aiglets in *or*, hands dorsed,
couped, crossed, clasped, bearing rings.
At her neck, a jewel, with diamonds cinquefoil,
enclosed by rubies and an emerald *vert*,
with a great pearl pendant, Above, a motto:
'Lady Mari, doughter to the most vertuous prince,
King Henri the Eight, the age of XXVIII yeres.'

Here is my courtly face, my carapace,
my gorgeous armoured shell, my shield:
see how my lips are pursed, my watchful eyes *en garde*,
and on the pearly chain linked round my throat
there hangs my father's latest gracious gift,
his badge, his mark, my jewelled submission
to that most paternal prince. For here I stand
like some heraldic beast, a captive emblem
of his resplendent state, emblazoned on
a cloudless backcloth, where my past is hid,
submerged in an empty sky of slate.

Still, I have made good master John paint
some subtle secret signs upon my shield:
my stifled heart bleeds out upon my sleeve
the rich vermillion of my early woes.
Despite the motto, I will never bear
bar sinister upon my name. White satin and
a choir of pearls sing out in truth

of my beloved mother's virtue and pure fame.
The tawny tinctures of my hair and robe
with richer reds, as vibrant as flame,
invoke her badge of Spain, and make me seem
a living fruit who yet will flower again.

Rosemary Mitchell

On Vermeer's Christ in the House of Martha and Mary
— For Hannah

Mustard-clad Martha, with her
white sleeves and warm loaf
bustles, bent over the bleached-
new linen of her tidy table.

Christ, cool, contemplative, in
muted plum and teal, reclines,
recommending Mary with
an elegant hand, drawing our focus.

The still and pensive Mary
at his feet, her billowing blue-
red shape, swelling, pregnant
with a purifying passion.

At her back, a decidedly Dutch
carpet binds her scarlet blouse
and the blue-green robe of Christ
against Martha's homely yellow.

Shall we conclude, that all this
mystic Passion and Desire, detached,
apart, still needs the solid back-cloth
of a sheltering roof and meal?

Rosemary Mitchell

Receipt Book of Lady Cleavage of Combe, for the Year of Our Lord, 1792

Item: for one corset newly mended with added side panels (the said corset being burst upon the occasion of my great quarrel with that harridan Lady Crawford when her pox-ridden spaniel hath piddled upon my puce gown):

To Mistress Esther Lumley, needlewoman, 1 shilling

Item: for the sound kicking of a Methodist preacher who most impudently compared me to Messalina:

To three dirty boys, names unknown, 6^d between them

Item: for services rendered (on sundry occasions, principally in my boudoir of a Sunday evening, most vigorously discharged):

To Roger Lustily, footman, 5 shillings

Item: for six volumes of the Rev Dr Josiah Soddingley's selected sermons (to be read by our housekeeper for the edification of our manservants and maidservants of a Sunday evening):

To Master Peter Pagination, Bookseller, one guinea

Item: for my eldest son and heir, Lutterworth Everley Ribblesdon Cleavage, a brace of pistols (that he may lie abed of a morning with the window wide and practise his shooting upon the undergardeners):

To Kiljoy and Potshot, gunsmiths to the Duke of Deddington, three guineas

Item: for my daughter, Clytemnestra Elizabeth Brunhilda, Lady Aardvark, a collection of silver paperknives, uncommonly sharp, to console her for the return of her husband Sir Basil from his antipodean estates and his most cruel accusation that she, a daughter of Combe, had consorted illicitly in his absence with a well-endow'd Irish military man, whose name I forget:

To the same, ten shillings

Item: to Captain Adain O'Doherty Flannery Quinn, for services rendered in my boathouse during the illness of my footman:

One penny

Item: for services to my aged aunt the Marquise de Tombola when she was stranded in Paris during the Terrors where most unfortunately her head was employed to adorn a spike:

To M. Henri de Coup, Morts-Vous-Aimez, a sovereign

Item: for spitting upon that runt and traitor, Mr Pitt, upon the late opening of Parliament:

Three beggars, with rampant bad breath, a penny each

Item: towards the rebuilding of Rakewell College, Oxford, to silence the Dean of that place of learning, who impertinently accuses my second son Salisbury Glasgow Piddelhampton Cleavage, undergraduate of that College, or arson during an unspecified orgy in Trinity term:

To the bursar of Rakewell, fifty pounds (and not a penny more!)

Item: to three sluttish wenches, who claim to have witnessed Salisbury setting fire to the curtains of his room (where these impudent harlots were seducing the poor innocent lad and his modest young friends):

To Betsey Beddown, Polly Pleaser, Meg Mauler, a shilling each

Item: to a scoundrelly old porter, who offered to confirm the wanton wenches' slanderous tale:

To Ted Toper, sixpence

Item: to pay the gambling debts of my eldest son and heir Lutterworth in London this season:

To the Lords Fleecem and Grabbit, Sir Wastrel Beesley, and Peter Patter, Esq., the sum of four hundred pounds, six shillings, and tuppence

Item: to succour the starving poor of Combe during this uncommon hard winter:

To our vicar, the Rev Theodore Tedium, sixpence

Item: to beautify my daughter Eunice Potentia Ermentrude Alexia upon her coming out this season, Dr Fermor's Firewater to burn off her spots, a cunningly quilted underbodice to fill out her lamentably flat bosom, and a wig of blond hair to disguise her bald patches:

To Mlle Disguise, chemist and beautifier, three guineas

Item: to bribe Sir Henry Shortcash, to wed my daughter Eunice upon the close of the season

To his sundry debtors, two hundred and fifty pounds

Rosemary Mitchell

Closed Monday, Winter Months

a gothic old barrack ... within as without, it was unique, rambling and incommodious
    — description of Oakwell House, in Charlotte Brontë's *Shirley*

I.

She loosens the strings of her bonnet,
peers up at medallions of canonical poets,
Shakespeare looking 'suave' and Milton 'serene.'
Sunlight glistens though purple and amber glass,
tinting her view of tidy gardens
where blossoms bob in the breeze.
Her friend invites her to take tea.

Years later, an uxorious arm circles her waist.
Gold twines round her small finger;
her belly heaves with legitimate pride
and unfamiliar hormones. She steadies her gaze
on the round portraits in the windows, wonders
if Currer Bell might one day be pictured among them.
Her husband urges her to sit and rest a while.

II.

Out of season, all I'm afforded
is an outsider's view, like a scullery maid
straining for a glimpse beyond the green baize.
Through leaded panes I spy the plain, deal back
of a lacquered cabinet, the tilt of a mirror
where no young lady frowns at wayward curls,
pinching pink into wan cheeks.

In the courtyard, near the portaloo,
men in hard hats, toting clipboards,
weigh up the potential of old laundries,

discuss ramps, fire doors, education centres.
No Bewick's birds here, but robins
stabbing sodden soil, trans-Pennine traffic roar
saturating the garden of remembrance.

The café's open. I pick up the local rag.
Robbers steals a taxi, Man charged with assault.
The wobbly table slops my coffee onto the plastic cloth;
I blot it with *Council wins 6.2 million for new road.*
Shortbread crumbs print buttery comments on the paper.
Births, marriages, deaths. Winterbottom, Clive, on 5th January, aged 86.
Asleep in Jesus' loving arms.

Hannah Stone

Collection

Mr Frick communes with his beauties,
admires Lady Peel's black hat ablaze with crimson feather,
her wrist and finger triple-bound with gems;
gazes at Lady Skipworth from whose bosom
sketchy roses sprout.

His wife interrogates him.
Why, my dear, must you have another one?
You already own Frances Duncombe, dripping pearls,
and Mrs Baker bursting from her fine fringed robe;
aren't these enough for you?

A man has his 'needs,' dearest, he replies,
his eyes on Mrs Elliot's beauty spot.
I thought we understood each other.
He thumbs the brocade of his waistcoat.
You have your interests; the quilting group,
a new title from the library subscription every month!

Mrs Frick spins on her heel; pleated silk
pinches a bunion. She glares at Lady Taylor,
whose eyes are blue as the cloudless sky,
and Lady Hamilton; notes her hectic cheeks
and how the glossy spaniel spills into her lap.

A log crumbles in the hearth beneath the el Greco,
the blaze lights up the tears quivering
in Mrs Frick's eyes. She breathes hard
under the steel ribs of her corset.

My dear, compose yourself, her husband begs.
You want for nothing: did you not care
for the trinkets I ordered from Chicago?

And the new nursemaid: I trust she gives
satisfaction to you, and the child?

Mrs Frick reflects. Beneath her bonnet,
each thought is whale-boned,
each whim pinned into place.
She cannot comprehend these women
with their flowing ribbons and loose bodices.

Mr Frick takes her hand.
I must have her, he states.
Mrs Hatchett, what a masterpiece!
Eyes wide beneath arched brows.
A bold mouth, clamped on secrets.
Curls cascading across her décolletage.

Her consort withdraws her fingertips,
nods stiffly, leaves the room.
There's a final dusting of the dado rail,
servants bustle off with the crate.
Wood shavings spin across the parquet.
The secretary enters to update the catalogue,
his nib squeaking a little in the quiet room.

Secured in her boudoir,
Mrs Frick replaces the stopper
in a flask of *sal volatile*.
On her walls, she hangs only landscapes.

Hannah Stone

The Conference Reception is Held in the Isabella Stewart Gardner Museum

After a long day of presentations,
the delegates have plenty to discuss.
Sloshed on Peach Bellinis
they screech amidst the ferns
that shade the courtyard pool.
Strains of Dvorak climb the creepers,
threading patterns through unglazed Moorish windows.

The shallow treads invite ascent.
A tipsy visitor joins a quieter colloquium on the *piano nobile*.
A Flemish matron, glazed into a wimple, gazes
at a beautiful boy as he springs from a sarcophagus.
A dozen Madonnas compare notes
on their holy joys and mysteries,
commiserate about their son's five wounds.

Stewards smile; they have no script.
The velvet ropes speak their restraint.
The guest climbs another flight of stairs,
saunters past many other treasures,
finds the portrait of their hostess
commanding a corner vantage point.
A small ocean of pearls girds her waist,
rides the swell of her hips.

The glass is empty now; the reception draws to a conclusion.
It is time for delegates to board buses, queue for elevators
to rooms where they kick shoes into corners, swirl into sleep.
It is time for Gainsborough's sheep
to stop nibbling; for Saint George to stay his stabbing hand;
for tapestries to relax into limp creases
and snuffboxes to switch off their enamel glow.

In the foyer, assistants pack glasses into boxes,
and the thousands of words smeared on their rims
begin to evaporate into the mock-Venetian night.

Hannah Stone

Rich Bride, or Christening Cake: Mrs Beeton Bakes

Ingredients: five pounds of finest flour –
not my own recipes, but I choose them well.
Currants washed, picked, and dried – so very
small and shining, like my many siblings
come warm and wriggling from the bath.
A fine Continental education for me, then
almonds pounded up with orange-water.
I marry sweet, chaotic Sam, my love
and equal. *The candied peel cut in neat
slices,* and our labours now begin. We
work the butter with the hand. I write,
translate French novels, *stir in the sugar*
in Sam's magazines. *Whisk the whites
to a solid froth* of light literature,
beat up the yolks and add the spice. I fold
myself in him, *beating the whole together.*
Add currants, almonds, wine and brandy here,
binding together the recipes of other cooks.
I season them well with tips on maids
and etiquette, and medicines, baking
my mixture *in a tolerably quick oven.* And so
my name was made, and Sam's poor papers
saved. But fate cut my cake *with a clean knife*
and took my sons, one by one. *Put on
a thick layer of almond icing, and one
of sugar too, for ornamentation.*
For in these icy days, I am with child again
and yet I fear. *Attention must be paid
to the heat of the oven: it should not be
too fierce. Time: five to six hours,* or
twenty-eight years? *And average cost:
two shillings per pound,* or all my short days?

Rosemary Mitchell

Pioneer Woman, or Prairie Queen

In dusk, dreaming, I see *delectable mountains*
and so decide – I will not be lashed to a man,
nor hemmed in by a white picket fence. Before dawn,
I will rise, put on furs and stout boots, go out
into the still air, and sew my own destiny
under a skyful of *stars*, a *wanderer's path*.
I will not bear you children, and bury some, and cook,
and clean, and bake bread, and number harsh years by
the pains in my back. I'll take your wagon, and the horse
who waits for me in the stable now, breathing steam like
a locomotive. I will see wide prairies
and high hills, eat grass perhaps, and starve a little
under hot suns, bathe naked in clear streams, run from the
bear's paw, watch flocks of birds pattern their path
across the spreading sky. And I will not despise
the dark, sure-footed people who have walked this land
before us, and know its *endless paths* by heart.
No, not even though they kill me. I will wear a gun
in my belt and my own mind in my head, and pass
through new worlds that tease me like *Solomon's puzzle*.
And I will fear nothing but the prisons of the soul
men build, the threads of a sullen spirit. So sleep,
as I slip from your bed, take off your ring, put on your
hat, and go to meet new days, a *Rose of Sharon*,
dewy in dawn *sun-burst*, free to walk my *crazy* ways.

Rosemary Mitchell

The Three Maries

The three Maries, resurrectionists in their own right,
prepare unctions and spices on a rough and tear-swept table.
Morning sun shoots lances of light through narrow windows,
bending a nimbus round each head. Their hands
caress the bodies of alabaster jars, squeezing
rich and rolling oils through tight necks. The air
is alive with aromas, heavy with the burden
of their love and grief.

Noli me tangere, says Christ, garbed as a gardener
bent on growing, risen, radiant, resuscitated.
A little fearful, perhaps, of an electric shock, if
touched by the Magdalene, pregnant with
her own peculiar intensity of life. For,
from his mother's womb, he was acquainted with
the swelling, terrifying power of women.

Rosemary Mitchell

A Say in Things

I. *A Women's Social and Political Union pin, belonging to Leonora Cohen, with Suffragette iconography*

I hold her in hand
on a smooth shining roundel,
a white woman, pinned.

A gate flung open,
she walks with doves, her chains dropped,
her drapery free.

Vocal in a scroll,
she demands the vote, changing
pale grey to wide green.

II. *An iron bar, probably from a fire grate, with a green luggage label, inscribed with a message ending 'Deeds, not Words.'*

A simple iron bar,
stolen from my lodgings,
is my sword of Justice.

Sheathed in my coat,
it bears a luggage label
with words to hit home.

Amid shining jewels,
I cast iron, shatter glass, and
so steel my own soul.

III. *A feeding tube, used to force-feed Suffragette prisoners on hunger strike.*

My body strapped down,
a steel gag rapes my mouth,
soundlessly open.

A tube tears my throat,
food fiercely floods my stomach:
I scream silently.

After the *gavage*,
retching, ravaged, I critique
state power in vomit.

IV. *A dress, featuring Suffragette iconography, created by Leonora*
Cohen and worn by her to the Leeds Arts Club ball in 1914.

In turquoise silk
with a sash of shields, I dress
for a local dance.

The humble tunic
is turned haughty, emblazoned
like a coat of arms.

Under our banner,
stern Justice still sweeps forward,
even as blue skies fall.

V. *A blue plaque, on a house in Clarendon Road, Leeds,*
commemorating the life and achievements of Leonora Cohen, who
lived there in the 1920s.

Blue plaque on red brick,
an ordinary terrace
in suburbia.

I live so long,
I grow respectable, a
Justice of the Peace.

Now I throw no stones,
but still wage war with words, which
petrify as deeds.

Rosemary Mitchell

Archaeology of a Sort

Max likes to dig things up,
fragments of a long-dead past
buried beneath hot sands,
in this sun-bleached, ancient place,

shaded by the cool makeshift walls
of the court in our Mesopotamian
house, while Arab boys whisper
to each other at the well.

I clean these old shards
with soft cloth and face-cream,
striving to reassemble them, fix
them forever in a photograph.

Max prefers them in full light,
no shadows to obscure their shapes.
But I prefer the play of shade on surface,
the sense of unsolved mystery in each empty pot.

For I like to bury things, corpses
and clues, deep in the dark places
of my books. Take the lie of my land,
when dusk's shade is aslant –

perhaps you will see the lines
which show how I filled *The Hollow*
with narrative distractions. In an old house
on the hillside, choked with bindweed,

you shine a torch, and see, beneath
the wallpaper, signs of a sealed door
and *Sleeping Murder*. In the gardens of
three sisters, pursued by *Nemesis,*

the glass of a ruined greenhouse
is suddenly lit by a late sun, and
you see the buried Verity.
My corpses may be long dead,

cobwebbed in mystery, but
Elephants Can Remember: they can
piece together fragments, weave a
terrible tapestry. Just so did

The Lady of Shalott, before
The Mirror Crack'd from side to side
and brought down on her the curse, the
crumbling brickwork clarity of it.

That lady had *An Appointment With Death*.
We all do, in some rose-red
city of stone, amidst the sinister shadow
of its streets and tombs. For burial's

the order of the day. No fear for me.
I've been burying myself my whole life.
In accidental amnesia, I once sat hidden in plain sight
in the shady window of a Harrogate hotel.

Rosemary Mitchell

Fenwick Lawson, Pietà, 1974-81, Elm

Northern pietà, not pretty,
cracked, bruised and broken
by the shapeless horror of
her son's sodden and shattered
body. Dishonoured, assailed,
rejected. Salvaged strangely
from lightning bolt at York,
but rain-raddled, rain-withered
in the courts of Durham. All flesh
is grass, all sculpture, too, decays,
and even the rood of life, slung over
sanctuaries, shall some day rot. Still,
God grows seed from death. And shape
breeds memory, pity, yearning to incarnate
the living sap – hard tears
the sculptor's hand struck off.

Rosemary Mitchell

Patricia

When you're a ninety-two year old Byzantinist,
the conference comes to you.
On a snowy evening, after the speeches,
I place a glass of red into trembling fingers,
and hold pretzels in a napkin
for you to peck at between anecdotes,
blowing crumbs at me as I bend my ear to your tale.

Sixty years of conference wool on your back,
you're no longer upright,
but your gaze is straight as an arrow,
and your eyes bright, now with fun,
as we agree being naughty is wasted on the young,
now with tears for your long gone husband.

An attendant daughter suggests I circulate,
but I'm hooked, swapping stories about Brussels,
(mine circa 1973, yours post-war),
and the joy of bearing children – and then it's time to part,
and I press a kiss onto the soft crenulations of your cheek.
Your history warms me as I pick a route
back over the crusted ice of a reluctant spring.

Hannah Stone

Umm Hoda

I'm used to wearing men's clothes now.
It's forty years since I last revealed any feminine curves:
back in the seventies concealment was the only way
to keep new suitors at bay. My husband
passed away three months before our daughter was born,
and my brothers were desperate to marry me off again,
make me somebody else's wife
before I'd even mourned my first man
or given life to our child.

What choice did I have?
I'd not been to school,
but I had the strength of ten men!
I shaved my hair off,
chose loose-fitting robes
because manual labour was the only way
I could provide for my daughter –
making bricks, harvesting wheat –
anything the men could do, I'd turn my hand to.

I disappeared from view,
though I never pretended to be what I wasn't.
In time, the whole of Luxor knew about me.
Umm Hoda, they called me, Hoda's Mum.

Umm Hoda gave up more than skirts.
I had to learn to think like a man;
that way, they accepted me as one of them.
After work we'd all go and drink coffee together.
No-one bothered me because I'd put aside my femininity;
back home, my brothers never forgave me.

Am I still labouring, you ask?
Well, these days I'm not so strong as I was,

so I've taken up shining shoes,
and the city chiefs gave me a kiosk
to shelter me from the weather.
I don't mind what I do,
as long as Hoda doesn't have to do what Hoda's mum does.
Her man's too ill to work,
so now I'm helping out so her kids can eat.

It was a proud moment when the President shook my hand
and gave me the award for being the most devoted mum.
One day, when I get time,
I'll ask Hoda to read me everything that's written
on the gilt-edged certificate.

Hannah Stone

Sacrament

'It was like a sacrament'
(Gate A4, Naomi Shihab Nye).

The spontaneous sharing
of homemade cookies,
broken and handed round –
it was like a sacrament.

The suspension of suspicion
of the other; the vision
of the woman behind the veil –
it was like a sacrament.

The care for the anxious stranger,
nourishing her with stuttered fragments
of a half-remembered mother tongue –
it was like a sacrament.

The skill of the poet, herself grafted
from warring communities,
stitching together the story –
it was like a sacrament.

Hannah Stone

We are not fools

We are not fools in Batley and Spen. I am proud that I was made in Yorkshire and I'm proud of the things we make in Yorkshire. We make beds and biscuits, carpets and lathes. We make the best fish and chips in the country. We make the best curries in the world. We are Fox's biscuits. We are an industrial heart wrapped in a very rich and pleasant Yorkshire landscape. We are Lion confectionary. We are Catholics from Ireland. We are not fools in Batley and Spen. We want reality behind the rhetoric of the Northern Powerhouse. Many of us want the stability of staying in Europe. We are Muslims from Gujarat and Kashmir. While we celebrate our diversity, what surprises me time and time again as I travel around the constituency is that we are far more united and have far more in common than that which divides us. We are not fools in Batley and Spen. Non-conformity is what we do best. We are not fools.

Hannah Stone

Sally Yates to a Malefactor of Great Wealth, or Speaking Truth to Power

I am responsible   *Feisty!*
I am responsible for ensuring   *Bossy!*
the positions we take in court   *Calm down dear!*
remain consistent   *One hysterical lady*
with this institution's obligations   *Needs a dressing down*
to always seek justice   *Just like a woman*
and stand for what is right   *Undressed with my eyes*

At present I am not convinced   *Just dress like a woman*
that the defence of the executive order   *You can try to silence*
is consistent with these responsibilities   *Heroic patriots*
nor am I convinced   *We cannot silence*
that the executive order   *Silence!*
is lawful.   *Silence in court!*

Hannah Stone

Life-Cycle: on My Late Mother's Charm Bracelet

It starts with a *Turtle*, ancient world-bearer
slow-rolling out your lifespan with a secret smile.
Destiny dictates, too, a *Spinning-Wheel*, where your humble
history's spun. No royal finger's pricked, though:
you're but a doctor's daughter, woven in Wales,
so here's a *Fleur-de-Lys*, a prince's feather for
your country, and a *Miner's Lamp* for your forbears.
Your grandfather struck black gold from a coal-face, and I recall
now that you hammered on a typewriter at the Coal Board
in the fifties. And here hangs a *Chimney-Sweep*, top-hatted
with his lucky ladder: a cheeky promise of fortune for a bride
on her wedding day. About the middle of the chain, a *Heart* is
fastened, close to a *Welsh Love-Spoon*, and a *Scout Hat*:
These three spell Dad. A green-tinted china *Tyrolean Hat*
hanging nearby, recalls with a porcelain clarity your holidays.
You ever loved a mountain – and a drink, the *Tankard* tells me.
And that *Leather Bottle*, did it once hold wine?
A *Silver Bird* swoops in, letter in beak: a message, perhaps
for the mother *Cow*? Sometime after I am born, the *Sled*
begins to slide downhill. But there's still *Leo*, your birth-sign:
you're brave of heart, and will rage against the dying
of *Green Light*. Towards the end, I see the signs of passing time,
a blue-flowered *Bell*, and a *Clock*, which ticks to termination
in a *Cathedral*'s shade. Your circle's closed; the charms
all told. I wrap and lock your bracelet in a chest,
secure you as soundly as I can in the *Round Tower*
of my weeping heart.

Rosemary Mitchell

Afterword

Mao Zedung once said that women hold up half the sky – the heavier half.

The impetus behind *Holding up Half the Sky* was the realisation that, throughout history, women's voices have been submerged, distorted or absent, through lack of education, conscious oppression, or simply a cultural context which denied them an opportunity to speak for themselves. In some areas of the world this is still very much the case.

The poems, stories and other texts in *Holding up Half the Sky* are germinations of our reading and discussions about a range of women's histories. They grow from the concept of 'found' poems, in the sense that the ideas and (in some cases) the actual words were taken from existing sources, not all of them printed. Many of them acknowledge that women – together with other less prestigious groups within the society of their day – created records of their experience which have been overlooked by history as they do not conform to the conventions normally ratified by the (usually male) elite.

Each piece has an identifiable source (which we have cited in the notes), but we have taken some liberties with the ideas, words and personae we encountered. The aim is always to bring to life narratives from women, to give a voice to their thoughts and stories, often through layers of meaning. In reading them you will bring yet another layer, that of your own reading and experience.

Hannah Stone and Rosemary Mitchell

Regina. A second-century AD tombstone found on Hadrian's Wall commemorates the native-born former slave and wife of a Syrian immigrant, Barathes.

Anonymous Figure, Ashmolean Museum. The 'handshake' depicted between the two male figures is the first one ever recorded. There was no further information about the woman.

Macrina. Sister and friend to the fourth century Cappadocian Fathers, Macrina embraced virginity on the death of her fiancé; she ran her household at Anessi on socially egalitarian lines.

The Empress Theodora, from her Bath. Procopius, in whose *Secret Histories* a highly redacted account of this sixth century Empress's life appears, records that the courtiers disapproved of her staying too long in the bath. Before she married Emperor Justinian she was a circus performer and sex worker.

Mary to Zosimas. The hermit Mary is the eponymous 'harlot' in Benedicta Ward's *Harlots of the Desert*. By convention in early Christian asceticism women were polarised as either saints or promiscuous sinners. The story somehow found its way from Syria to Anglo-Saxon England where it was translated into Old English.

Syrian Mary to her Fallible Uncle. This story is also in *Harlots of the Desert*.

A Troubled Seer Writes to Bernard of Clairvaux. Hildegard of Bingen (1098-1179) was a German Benedictine Abbess, visionary, mystic and composer, honoured as the founder of a scientific approach to natural history.

A Shewing in Which I am Nourished by Milk from Jesus' Breasts. Julian of Norwich was a fourteenth-century hermit. Her *Visions of Divine Love*, depicting the 'shewings' of God to her on her sickbed, is reputedly the first recorded writing by a woman in England. Her use of feminine imagery to describe God predated the norm in western Christianity by 600 years.

British Library MS Additional 61823: a Partial Chronology. The *Book of Margery Kempe*, possibly one of the earliest female autobiographies, lay undiscovered for centuries after being written down by amanuenses in the fifteenth century.

The Duchess's Double: On the effigy of Alice Chaucer, Duchess of Suffolk. Alice Chaucer (grand-daughter of the poet) was Duchess of Suffolk. Her tomb in Ewelme church is the only example of a transi or cadaver tomb for a woman

Queen Anne commends herself to Saint Margaret of Antioch. A Netherlandish *Book of Hours*, c. 1500 shows Saint Margaret of Antioch reading her psalter, attended by a dragon, an image associated with childbirth as – according to the legend – her cross caused the dragon which ate her to regurgitate her.

1544: Her Grace, in a Table. This poem refers to a portrait of Princess Mary commissioned in 1544. The references to heraldry allude to her illegitimate status.

Receipt Book of Lady Cleavage of Combe, for the Year of Our Lord, 1792. Lady Cleavage is an imaginary aristocrat, frustrated by the limitations of her gender and bothered by family responsibilities.

Collection. The Frick Collection in New York was gathered by industrialist Henry Clay Frick (1849-1919). Several rooms are devoted to portraits of alluring society women.

The Conference Reception is Held at the Isabella Stewart Gardner Museum. Isabella Stewart Gardner (1840-1924) was a leading American collector and philanthropist, who commissioned a mock Venetian palace to house her artefacts.

Pioneer Woman, or Prairie Queen. The words in italics are the names of quilt patterns used by American pioneer women.

The Three Maries. The 'text' for this was a Station of the Cross in St Chad's Chapel, University of Durham.

A Say in Things. Leonora Cohen (1873-1978) was a prominent Leeds Suffragette. Her mother, a widowed seamstress, told her daughter things would improve if they 'had a say in things.'

Archaeology of a Sort. Agatha Christie (1890-1976) is best known as a crime writer, as indicated by the italicised titles of her books. She was married to archaeologist Max Mallowen and assisted on his archaeological digs in the Middle East. In

1926, suffering from amnesia, she disappeared for ten days.

Patricia. Written in memory of Patricia Karlin-Hayer (d. 2014), who was a translator of Byzantine texts, scholar, cook, mother, grand-mother and story-teller.

Umm Hoda. The 'found' element in Umm Hoda is an article from *The Guardian*, 23 March, 2015. 'Sisa Abu Saooh – Egyptian woman who lives as a man – voted 'best mum.''

Sacrament. The line 'It was like a sacrament' from Naomi Shihab Nye's poem **Gate A4** is cited by kind permission of the poet. Her poem is an account of an incident at Albuquerque Airport, involving homemade mamool cookies.

We are Not Fools. Quotations are taken from the maiden speech of MP for Batley and Spen, Jo Cox, delivered on 3 June, 2015. Jo Cox was murdered in her constituency on 16 June, 2016.

Sally Yates to a Malefactor of Great Wealth, Speaking Truth to Power. The words of sacked Attorney General Sally Yates' speech about the ban on Muslim immigration are interrupted by interjections from Theodore Roosevelt, David Cameron, Donald Trump, and Zac Petkanas.

Indigo Dreams Publishing Ltd
24, Forest Houses
Cookworthy Moor
Halwill
Beaworthy
Devon
EX21 5UU
www.indigodreams.co.uk